In
1935 if you wanted to
read a good book, you needed
either a lot of money or a library card.
Cheap paperbacks were available, but their
poor production generally mirrored the quality
between the covers. One weekend that year,
Allen Lane, Managing Director of The Bodley Head,
having spent the weekend visiting Agatha Christie,
found himself on a platform at Exeter station trying to
find something to read for his journey back to London.
He was appalled by the quality of the material he had to
choose from. Everything that Allen Lane achieved from that
day until his death in 1970 was based on a passionate belief
in the existence of 'a vast reading public for *intelligent*
books at a low price'. The result of his momentous vision
was the birth not only of Penguin, but of the 'paperback
revolution'. Quality writing became available for the price of
a packet of cigarettes, literature became a mass medium
for the first time, a nation of book-borrowers became a
nation of book-buyers – and the very concept of book
publishing was changed for ever. Those founding
principles – of quality and value, with an overarching
belief in the fundamental importance of reading –
have guided everything the company has
done since 1935. Sir Allen Lane's
pioneering spirit is still very much alive
at Penguin in 2005. Here's to
the next 70 years!

# MORE THAN A BUSINESS

'We decided it was time to end the almost customary half-hearted manner in which cheap editions were produced – as though the only people who could possibly want cheap editions must belong to a lower order of intelligence. We, however, believed in the existence in this country of a vast reading public for intelligent books at a low price, and staked everything on it'
**Sir Allen Lane, 1902–1970**

'The Penguin Books are splendid value for sixpence, so splendid that if other publishers had any sense they would combine against them and suppress them'
**George Orwell**

'More than a business ... a national cultural asset'
**Guardian**

'When you look at the whole Penguin achievement you know that it constitutes, in action, one of the more democratic successes of our recent social history'
**Richard Hoggart**

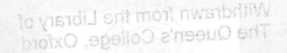

# Protobiography

WILLIAM BOYD

PENGUIN BOOKS

PENGUIN BOOKS

Published by the Penguin Group
Penguin Books Ltd, 80 Strand, London WC2R ORL, England
Penguin Group (USA) Inc., 375 Hudson Street, New York, New York 10014, USA
Penguin Group (Canada), 10 Alcorn Avenue, Toronto, Ontario, Canada M4V 3B2
(a division of Pearson Penguin Canada Inc.)
Penguin Ireland, 25 St Stephen's Green, Dublin 2, Ireland
(a division of Penguin Books Ltd)
Penguin Group (Australia), 250 Camberwell Road, Camberwell, Victoria 3124,
Australia (a division of Pearson Australia Group Pty Ltd)
Penguin Books India Pvt Ltd, 11 Community Centre,
Panchsheel Park, New Delhi – 110 017, India
Penguin Group (NZ), cnr Airborne and Rosedale Roads, Albany,
Auckland 1310, New Zealand (a division of Pearson New Zealand Ltd)
Penguin Books (South Africa) (Pty) Ltd, 24 Sturdee Avenue,
Rosebank 2196, South Africa

Penguin Books Ltd, Registered Offices: 80 Strand, London WC2R ORL, England

www.penguin.com

First published without 'The Hothouse' by The Bridgewater Press 1998
'The Hothouse' first published in *School Ties* by Penguin Books 1985
This selection published as a Pocket Penguin 2005

1

Copyright © William Boyd, 1985, 1998
All rights reserved

The moral right of the author has been asserted

Set in 10.5/12.5pt Monotype Dante
Typeset by Palimpsest Book Production Limited
Polmont, Stirlingshire
Printed in England by Clays Ltd, St Ives plc

# Contents

Preface                           1

Fly Away Home                     4

The Lion Griefs                   11

The Hothouse                      26

Memories of the Sausage Fly       49

# Preface

Having always classed myself – quite deliberately – as a resolutely un-biographical writer, it came as something of a surprise to discover there was in fact one area of my life that I had documented with some thoroughness: namely my early childhood in Africa and my schooldays at a boarding school in Scotland. One explanation for this may be that, as we grow older, there is an unconscious urge to log these early experiences before amnesia intervenes or the rose-tinted glasses of nostalgia alter the picture forever. I know this was a key motive for writing about boarding school, which I first did at some length in my book *School Ties*, appending a memoir of my almost-ten years in a single-sex boarding school as an introduction to my two film scripts about public school life, 'Good and Bad at Games' and 'Dutch Girls'. I wanted, quite simply, to tell the truth before I forgot – but I was more interested in telling the truth about the institution rather than exposing anything particularly revelatory about myself.

These four pieces here, however, do have the author unequivocally at centre stage. The two about West Africa were published some ten years apart. 'Memories of the Sausage Fly' appeared in the *London Review of Books* and 'Fly Away Home' was included in an anthology edited by Caryl Phillips (in 1997) called *Extravagant Strangers* – a collection of pieces about first impressions of Britain. Neither would have been written without the encouragement of the editors – Caryl Phillips himself and Mary Kay Wilmers at the *LRB* – as I felt no personal impulse to tell the respective stories at all. But, looking back at these reflections now, I realize that I am particularly grateful to them both for their prompting, for giving me the space and allowing me the opportunity. 'The Lion Griefs', however, was written especially for this volume, expanding considerably on a short essay for a privately printed *festschrift* celebrating the fifty-year anniversary of my junior prep school, Wester Elchies. 'The Hothouse' is extracted from the introduction I wrote for *School Ties*. They seemed to me the ideal complement – a substantial bit of Scottish meat, as it were, in a predominantly African sandwich.

I have called this little book *Protobiography* as much to reflect the somewhat haphazard nature of its composition as to underscore the modest nature of the personal history it contains. I can't imagine ever writing an autobiography, so I suspect that anyone curious about my life will have to make do with these and similar gleanings. I have a theory that, for the novelist, the area of his or her life which is of most interest and real value, in terms of raw material, is that period of existence *before* you begin to think self-consciously of yourself as a writer, or at least before this ambition has come to the forefront of your conscious mind. In my own case this moment arrived in my early twenties and, when such a self-consciousness – such a self-dramatization – occurs, everything experienced subsequent to it is subtly but profoundly changed.

Everything becomes filtered, screened, analysed, pondered over. All the things that happen to you are transformed, sooner or later, into grist for the novelist's mill.

It strikes me that with *Protobiography* I have covered that area of ground pretty thoroughly, and I find myself wondering if I will ever write about myself in such an unimpeded way again.

# Fly Away Home

York, Hermes, Argonaut, Stratocruiser, Super Constellation, Britannia, Boeing 707, VC 10 . . . The story of my early encounters with England is a small history of aviation. I do not remember the York, a development of the Lancaster bomber, I believe, but in 1952 – the year I was born – my flying life began, in a Hermes. I was born in March in the Ridge Hospital in Accra, the capital of the Gold Coast. Four months later I was carried up the steps to the waiting Hermes to begin my first flight from my native land back to the place my parents came from. The Hermes followed the York on the first passenger services from Gold Coast to London, making a series of short hops across the great protruding bulge of Western Africa – Accra, Lagos, Kano, Tripoli – before crossing the Mediterranean to Madrid, Rome or Frankfurt and then on to London. The whole journey took seventeen hours.

I do remember the Argonaut quite well, however, a British version of the DC 6, a four-engined prop plane that did not owe anything to World War II precursors and was the first to make the trans-Sahara overfly routine (if one discounts the truly terrifying turbulence), and was thus able to cut the time of the West Africa to London trip substantially. We would land in Kano in northern Nigeria to refuel before setting off on the long leg over the desert to Tripoli. Kano airport was so fly-infested that the airport buildings were proofed with mosquito wire. Vultures perched on the control tower. We always crossed the

Sahara at night (perhaps at the level the planes flew in those days the turbulence made it impassable when the sun was up?) and we would arrive at Tripoli as dawn broke. For this reason Tripoli airport always seemed dramatic and somewhat disturbing to me, as I recall: its hangars were colandered from World War II shrapnel and in the pale light you could see cannibalized hulks of Italian bombers of the same era rusting mysteriously in the thin blond grass that fringed the runways. Beyond the perimeter fence camels grazed . . . There was still one more stop to be made in mainland Europe before we cruised over the English Channel to land at London airport – as Heathrow was always quaintly referred to in those days.

The Stratocruiser represented the ultimate in luxury. Twin-decked, with a glassy round bulbous nose, the plane tried to simulate the elegance of the Pullman cars in transcontinental express trains. Seats were arranged in fours, pairs facing each other. Above our heads was a reach-me-down bunk bed for children. On the lower deck was a small bar accessed by a tight spiral staircase, which I remember my parents descending for a cocktail before the meal was served – a side of roast beef on a silver trolley, the steward carving slices off it as if he were for all the world in the Savoy Grill and not twenty thousand feet above the dark wadis and sand seas of the endless Sahara.

All these aeroplanes and their successors – the Britannia, the VC 10, and so on – were in the livery of BOAC – the British Overseas Airways Corporation – crisp white and navy blue and badged with the famous speedbird logo (now long vanished). As I grew older and became conscious of our annual trips back to Britain on leave, the planes, and by extension the company, came to represent the country by proxy, as if a little segment of Britain had been sent out to the colonies to fetch us back to the mother-land. It was a kind of idealized metaphor, I suppose – the smart modern planes and their smart modern crew luring us on board with their smiles and their trays of boiled sweets – showing us what we had left behind, reminding us of our good fortune in being able to return.

My early experience of air travel instilled in me a love of flying, of airports and all the accoutrements of avia-tion which has not left me to this day. How could such an introduction to flight, at such an impressionable age, and with such magnificent ambassadors, not fail to entrance? As children our idea of a treat was to be driven from home to Accra airport to look at the BOAC plane. One runway, one uneven expanse of tarmac apron, a control tower, a few hangars, some low sheds doubling as immigration and customs, arrival and departure halls, Accra airport was modest and unassuming in the extreme. Across the road from the airport was the airport hotel, called The Lisbon for some forgotten reason, a single-storeyed wooden build-ing with a wide verandah. On Saturday nights a highlife band would play and the more daring young expatriate couples would come there to dance. Like all airport hotels in Africa it effortlessly maintained a louche and faintly racy ambiance. We children would take our drinks – our Fantas and Cokes – and go and stand at the wood paling fence and stare at the silver giant, propellers stilled, parked on the tarmac. Fuel bowsers and generators hummed, linked trolleys bouncing with luggage trundled from the depar-ture lounge, engineers and cleaners ran up and down the wheeled steps set against the doorways. Then came the crew, then came the long lines of passengers. Doors were closed, propellers turned, the plane was freed of its vari-ous appurtenances and it taxied to the end of the runway.

To see it lift off and climb into the dusty evening air was both exhilarating and melancholy, emotions perhaps not fully comprehended then but more easily analysed now. It has to be understood that in the Fifties, certainly from an African perspective, these tremendous aeroplanes, and the world they both encompassed and conjured up, were for us a vision of immense and modern glamour and at the same time, like all people being left behind, we felt a sense of flatness and disappointment lingering as we returned to the car and were driven home, counting the weeks and months until it would be our turn to cross that cracked uneven piste towards the blue and white flying machine and be carried away by it also, cosseted and nourished, across the desert to Europe, to England, homeward.

As you mounted the steps towards the door, almost swooning with excitement, the first impression, aside from the stewardess (a figure of unearthly exoticism), was olfactory. The smell of the flyspray that was liberally pumped throughout the plane's interior prior to take off was both sweet and oddly choking. It was a smell replicated nowhere else in my range of nasal memory – part marzipan, part cough medicine, part liqueur, part candy, part liniment . . . I could not place it: our flysprays at home did not smell remotely the same. But whatever it was, whatever brand it was or compound of chemical meeting unnatural fabric in a confined space, the BOAC version was potent and palpable. It was always, for me at least, the first smell of England. It was a kind of Rubicon; as you stepped over the threshold and were directed down the aisle, your lungs were filled with this curious reek. You soon became used to it but it signalled that your journey home had truly begun.

And yet my real home was in West Africa, in the Gold Coast – which in 1957 became Ghana. Until my tenth year

I only spent summers in Britain, almost always in Scotland. But my parental home was in Ghana, and so were my bedroom, my things, my school, my friends. Scotland was where my relatives lived, where we rented a house and my parents caught up with their families. We were always in transit, welcomed but always 'just visiting'. The real business of my life lay at the end of another plane journey in the reverse direction. And the comparative brevity of the annual leave never allowed us fully to integrate, to take things for granted, to become *au fait* with the latest fads and fashions. Little details remind me now of that sense of apartness. I felt ill at ease walking past school playgrounds, always stared at. Why wasn't this boy (me) at school? (one could sense the unspoken question). How were my sullenly curious coevals to know that African school holidays did not coincide with the British? If I had not detoured, I crossed the street, head down. I never felt comfortable with children of my age group, en masse. I remember my father too, a man of status and real importance on the university campus where he ran a hospital and health clinics responsible for 20,000 people, fumbling like a new immigrant with his unfamiliar change as he tried to buy a newspaper in Edinburgh. You could sense the newsagent's impatience building as my father picked and prodded hesitantly at a palmful of coins. I possessed also a vague embarrassment about my clothes. The shorts and sandals and shirts made from local tie-dyed cloth – which were wholly unexceptional in Ghana – seemed eccentric, not to say bizarre, in breezy St Andrews or the High Street in Peebles. I had no long trousers at all, and how I coveted my first pair of jeans – finally bought at the age of nine with an aunt in a department store in Birmingham – at last, knees covered, I might not stand out from the crowd. Needless to say I never felt like this in Africa, where I roamed about the countryside, cycled through the streets and boulevards of the enormous, sprawling campus, possessing the place so thoroughly, so intimately, that such unreflecting familiarity has never been reproduced, no matter where I have subsequently lived. I knew paths through the bush, short cuts through servants' quarters. I knew where the biggest mangoes grew, the best spot to catch pythons, what pie dogs to avoid, how to eat fufu, who would sell you a single stick of chewing gum, what were the rules and penalties of a complicated game involving the spinning of hollow snail shells . . . My life in Africa up until the age of ten was a modest but genuine idyll and its basic elements will be familiar to anyone who has grown up in the tropics – the child, the white child, still possessed a form of tolerant *laisser passer* denied the adult. We were unnoticed, or barely noticed, everywhere – which, when freedom to come and go is all you ask, is the best and most sincere form of welcome.

And then June came round and the rainy season threatened and it was time to go on leave. BOAC would send one of its planes to fetch us and the strange and exciting process that led to our landfall in England would begin. Sunset in Kano, the lurching rollercoaster of the night flight across the Sahara, dawn in Tripoli, morning in Madrid or Rome – finally peering through clearing clouds at the green patchwork of English fields and the occasional wink of sunburst from a car's windscreen. London airport. More low wooden buildings. Lino and formica. Tall blue policemen. Pale pasty faces. Strange accents . . . And somewhere, deep inside me, the private hollow of fear and insecurity that all aliens (however legal) carry within them. My passport was British so why was I uneasy?

It all changed when I was sent to boarding school in Scotland, something that happened to all expatriate children, as inevitable as puberty. However, my routine was turned on its head, everything was reversed: now I flew to Africa in the holidays. My family, my home, my room, my things, my friends were all as they had always been but now I only saw them for two months of the year. But back in Britain I was beginning to understand the place; I was beginning to be assimilated; I had started to fit in.

I was barely four months old when I made that first flight in a Hermes from Africa to England in 1952. My parents took me up to Scotland to present me to my grandmothers and the rest of the family. For some reason my father went back early and my mother and I joined him some weeks later at the end of our leave. By curious chance, as we were waiting in London airport for our plane to be called, there was a photographer from the *Evening Standard* patrolling the departure lounge looking for a light-hearted filler, I suppose, a bit of human interest for a corner of a page, snapping babes in arms about to go on a long plane journey, still a rarish event in those days, no doubt. My mother has kept the cutting. In the picture one glum and tearful toddler sits morosely on her mother's knee. Opposite is me, aged six months, fizzing with energy, bald and beefy as a Buddha, beaming hugely, my mother's arm clamped around my middle trying to stop the thrashing and the squirming. 'Why is master William Andrew Murray Boyd so happy?' the caption asks. I could not answer then, but I can now – I was flying home.

# The Lion Griefs

I went to boarding school at the age of nine. This was not exceptional: when I arrived at my school in September 1961 I found boys of six and seven. One exceptionally tiny boy – tawny-skinned with crow-black, dead-straight hair (was he half-Chinese?) – was rumoured to be five, though he angrily denied it.

I was not unhappy to be going away to school. In West Africa, where my parents lived, all the children of expatriate Europeans were doing the same at around my age. It was entirely normal and for years we were gently prepared (a form of benign brain-washing, I suppose) for the day when we would be left to fend for ourselves. Neither of my parents had been to public school or boarding school and both were unfamiliar with where or how to introduce me into the system. In the end it was decided that I should go to the same school as had a son of close friends. They had heard good reports of it; it was not horrifically expensive; I had seemed to like the place when I had been interviewed one summer when we were back on leave and, as I was Scottish, it was an advantage that the school was in Scotland, albeit in the remote far north. This northerly aspect provided the school with a not entirely deserved reputation for a Spartan, no-frills style of education, its most obvious manifestation being a proclaimed fondness for cold showers and early morning runs and the odd fact that the boys wore shorts throughout their school career, regardless of the seasons and the weather, until they left, aged eighteen.

The main school was serviced by two prep schools: the junior for boys up to the age of ten and a senior for boys from ten to thirteen who then, if they passed an undemanding entrance exam, were claimed by the parent institution. It was to the junior school that I was driven that September afternoon by my mother, all the way from Edinburgh, to find the field in front of the school house filled with forty or fifty small boys, dressed in navy blue jerseys and shorts, running about, kicking balls, wrestling and generally horsing around. It seemed like fun and I was oblivious to my mother's brimming tears as she said goodbye. She told me later she had had to stop outside the school gates, had pulled the car in to the side of the road and wept for an hour.

The junior prep school was housed in a former shooting lodge called Wester Elchies (now sadly demolished), a rather magical-looking Scottish baronial building with turrets and castellation set in fair-sized grounds with its own home farm. There were extensive woods, a telescope-less observatory and a curling pond. Over the hill was an orphanage (we were terrified of the orphans – sinister yahoos to our over-privileged eyes) and not far away, in the valley below, the River Spey flowed where salmon were caught by our headmaster, a legendary fly-fisher.

I was introduced to my 'minder', a tall rather glamourous blond boy called Holland. Holland was rich (his father had a Rolls-Royce) and he had an older brother who played in a pop group. This was a stroke of luck for me as, with Holland's patronage, I was introduced to his 'set' and achieved almost instant acceptance into the relatively innocent, tribal world of a prep school.

We were not particularly cruel to each other at this stage of our scholarly life, cruelty (sometimes exceptionally vicious) came later, after puberty, at the main school. For the pre-adolescent there seems to me to be only one requirement for success at prep school and that is popularity. Academic and sporting achievements at that age are so ephemeral and inconsequential that they gain little kudos, and at Wester Elchies the only miserable boys I recall were the unpopular ones. They were unpopular because they looked peculiar: Webster had the aspect of a puppet or cartoon character – with thick, springy carrot-coloured hair and heavy black specs; Sedley had dark, bruised eyes and unusually dun, greasy skin. Sedley was genially and routinely persecuted because he cried so easily. All it took was three or four of us to gather round him making quacking duck-bill movements with our hands and chanting 'Baitey! Baitey! Baitey!' and Sedley would obligingly break down into incoherent and hysterical weeping fits. We found this very amusing and never tired of the game. It was gratuitous but not malevolent. I don't think life at prep school as I experienced it was ever malign. The school's regime was good-natured, on the whole, the staff kind and tolerant. Sex and power, the two elements in boarding school life that really corrupt, even to the extent that they can make people evil, were waiting for our older selves up ahead.

Life at an all-boy prep school, though unreal (as all monosexual societies must be, by definition), was still an extension of childhood, and consequently our ambitions and disappointments, our desires and our hatreds retained some quality of childhood innocence. Most of our carnal energies, for example, were expended in trying to see female members of staff in the nude or, second best, to find some way of peering up into the dark recesses of their skirts. I and many others nurtured simultaneous passions for Miss Grey, the art teacher, and Miss Cibber, the music teacher. Miss Grey was tall and languorous with glossy dark hair wound round her head in a loose Bloomsburyesque bun. Her clothes were rich-looking, romantically hued. Miss Cibber too was dark, almost swarthy in fact, with a sturdier more curvaceous figure. For a term she ousted Miss Grey from my fantasies as I found myself allotted to a dormitory outside one of the staff bathrooms which she used. There was an inch-wide crack between the bottom of the door and the floor through which, if you pressed your head to the cold linoleum of the corridor, you could obtain a partial view of the bathroom beyond. Miss Cibber's strong legs from the thigh down became very familiar. We kept praying she would drop a towel or her toothbrush and have to bend over. She excluded herself from all our affections when she was surprised one day in a passionate kiss with the English master – a dull, weak fellow, to our eyes – called Hearn.

We did not like Hearn and therefore could not like anyone who liked him. Our affections were extremely fickle. Miss Cibber was dropped and I returned my loyalty to Miss Grey.

Ah, Miss Grey, Miss Catriona Grey! Strange how passionate the pre-pubertal crush can be. She must have been very young, in her early twenties, I suppose, and, as I recall her face, I realize she was very pretty too. I was good at art and saw a lot of her and became something of a favourite. Because I was close to her it is with Miss Grey that I associate my first adult feelings of envy – a pure, elemental, resentment-driven emotion. Miss Grey's beauty was not just apparent to her acolytes in the art room: the headmaster, Mr Vaughan, was also susceptible.

I was impressed by Mr Vaughan: he was the first person

whom I recognized – unconsciously – as 'sophisticated'. He drove an MG roadster with leather straps holding down the bonnet. He wore suede shoes, he smoked a lot, Player's Navy Cut, and had a deep, raspy smoker's voice. I can recall his flat in the school house with real clarity. A dark blue carpet, loose cream lineny covers on the sofas, good pictures on the walls. He was, I now realize, genuinely urbane, a confirmed bachelor, a throwback figure from John Buchan or Sapper who had taken up schoolmastering before the war in the way that young men did coming down from Varsity with a poor degree (think of Waugh and Auden) and had been too lazy, or found the life too congenial, ever to move on. He was white-haired – in his fifties – and being headmaster of a small prep school in Banffshire was to be the pinnacle of his professional life. But he seemed perfectly content and he used regularly to invite Miss Grey (a fellow smoker) to share a cigarette with him at his table at the end of the midday meal.

I can conjure up the tableau now, and the green fog of envious bile through which I viewed it, as we filed out to go to our dormitories for the obligatory postprandial rest. Mr Vaughan would push his chair back so he could cross his legs and dangle one brown suede shoe. He smoked with a small flourish, his hand describing a generous arc, a flexing, cuff-shooting movement, as he brought the cigarette to his lips. Inhaling avidly, laughing, leaning forward to share a throaty smoky confidence with Miss Grey who, her body language tells me in hindsight, was not wholly at ease with Mr Vaughan's raffish innuendoes. Miss Grey stiffly upright, an arm crossed below her breasts, a palm supporting the elbow of the smoking hand, the cigarette more demurely, more delicately, puffed at – a social smoker, then, not with Mr Vaughan's nicotine craving. I can hear

Mr Vaughan's barking laugh crossing the emptying dining room as we troop out, degenerating into a barking lung-tearing cough. I look back, hating him, wanting to kill him, to see Miss Grey leaning forward, helping him to a consoling glass of water.

What kind of person was I then, in my pre-teens? Memories are vivid and precise but I cannot summon up a retrospective self-consciousness. The world is a simpler more straightforward place when you are ten, eleven, twelve. It is adolescence, the burgeoning hormone-swarm in the body, that brings home real intimations of character and personality. I look at pictures of the fair-haired lad I was and gain no real access to the persona. The alternately carefree and moody fifteen-year-old, say, – both precocious and deeply lazy – is far more familiar. And yet the pre-teen places and the people, the events and the adventures lurk in the memory bank pristine and available.

I was popular, thanks partly to Holland and his cronies, and I was tall and a fast runner – did not let the side down at rugby and cricket – but I realize I never made it into the first rank because I did not have a nickname. The real stars were called 'Ducky' or 'Fitzy' or plain 'Johnnie'. Once for a week or so a few boys took to calling me a latinate 'Boydus' but it never caught on and soon died away, never to be resurrected. What made these boys so liked, what was the secret of their charm, so evident that even the staff addressed them by their nicknames? The answer, I think, is that they were unrelentingly cheerful. As they became teenagers they seemed almost visibly to fade away, without exception, puberty robbing them of their unfailingly sunny demeanours. But somehow at the age of ten or eleven an initial personality had developed, sufficient to make them the life and soul of the party, and this was enough to make them everybody's favourites. These boys were loved, admired and cherished, I am sure, by all of us without any jealousy. I remember when 'Johnnie's' mother suddenly died the sense of collective grief in Elchies was palpable: his loss affected us all in a profound way that can only be explained by the role he played in our midst. Johnnie's loss was, of course, our loss too.

Indeed, within the small community of the prep school a kind of covert favouritism operates, rather as I imagine it does in a large family, with no real resentment being expressed by those excluded. For a while I was the beneficiary of such advancement when I became the favourite of the matron – I think as a result of having suffered a very bad dose of chicken pox – Mrs Herrick, a pallid but no-nonsense, vivacious woman, married to the Latin teacher (we called him 'Shirley' for some forgotten reason). Mrs Herrick was not the most powerful patron among the staff, but her benevolence did pay dividends.

Every morning – part of our Scottish heritage – we had porridge for breakfast. The school would gather in the assembly room before filing through to the dining room (a pre-fab wooden hall tacked on to the rear of the house). Mr Vaughan would declaim a prayer, read the day's notices and then Mrs Herrick would appear to select the sugar-server. This was one of the most coveted jobs in the school (our sweet ration was one Quality Street per day). The sugar-server's job was to place one dessertspoonful of brown Demerara sugar in the middle of each bowl of porridge. The key perk of the job was that one was permitted to sugar one's own bowl of porridge with boundless liberality. And, naturally, friends of the sugar-server benefited also. During my reign as Mrs Herrick's chosen-one she would come into the assembly room each morning, scan the eager pleading faces of the boys and then, as if the result of spontaneous whim, select me. This went on for many weeks and nobody ever appeared to express surprise or complain at this manifest unfairness. I became rather smug and developed a sweet tooth that I have never really managed to neutralize.

My move to prep school from my school in Africa meant the first of several progressive steps that shifted me away from being an 'African' child to becoming a British one. The winter of 1961 was the first time I saw snow. As I remember it there had been a heavy fall in the night, some six inches or so, and we woke to the refulgent, muffled, eerie landscape that dense snowfall brings. For two of us – me and another boy who had been born and raised in Jamaica – this was a surreal lifetime first. Amazed, astonished, we stepped outside and picked the stuff up, tasted it, felt its cold numb our fingers, heard its crump beneath our feet. Other boys and staff, amused, looked out at us from the big library windows – two aborigines out of their element – as we struggled to come to terms with this new natural phenomenon that we had heard and read so much about but never experienced – stamping our feet, throwing handfuls into the air – before we were gently summoned back inside for breakfast.

Quite a number of us lived abroad and made the long plane journey home at holidays – to India, West and East Africa, Singapore, the Caribbean – to a world of sun and humidity, ocean beaches and palm trees. On our return we wore our exclusivity proudly in the shower room, our deep tans contrasting strongly with the pale pink bodies of our coevals, quite unconcerned to be known to the others as 'wogs'. This sort of cheery racism was quite common, even at prep school, but, as with many of the less admirable aspects of boarding school life, our prejudices and bigotries tended to become more extreme as we grew older. Any deviation from our self-ordained norms was more mercilessly pilloried – accents, deformities, perceived ugliness – anything strange or out of the ordinary was grist to the intolerance mill.

But at the junior prep school our energies and animosities revolved instead around the forts we built in the woods. This was a form of peer-group-creation, joining a gang combined with war-gaming, a kind of obsessive militaristic territoriality that dominated our free time. Who was in, who was out, whose loyalties had been transferred and so on. In the dense woods around the house we would build elaborate shacks, lean-tos and tree houses, erect earthworks and construct trip wires and booby traps. Membership of the most splendid forts was eagerly striven-for. Certain substantial forts of the recent past had assumed almost legendary proportions. There had been one called 'Laramie' – but somehow Laramie had fallen into disrepair and all that remained of it was a jumble of roped-together logs in a clearing. Old hands would take new boys to the site and reminisce about its Ozymandian splendours.

One was elected into a fort either by patronage (Holland helped me into his) or by the possession of tools. In this way feeble or unpopular boys could gain admission into elites by offering the use of a hammer or drill or, in one enterprising case, by having his father send up supplies of six-inch nails at weekly intervals. The six-inch nail was the key currency – you could buy your way anywhere.

The move to the senior prep school, a few miles away on the other side of the Spey, marked an end to the Edenic pleasures of the Wester Elchies. The new house was grander and larger, with a great pillared portico, a stable block and generous formal terraces leading down to playing fields. It represented a larger society, too, and within it were played out early and inchoate strategies of power and responsibility, and with that development came a corresponding loss of innocence. Here were thirteen-year-olds in the first hot flush of adolescence, voices breaking, pimples sprouting, the first snouty stirrings of pubertal lust. The easy egalitarianism of the junior school ebbed away, the sense of being part of a large, unruly but essentially loving family was replaced by the divisions familiar to all closed societies. There was the public face of the school – sporty, academic, disciplined – and there was the inevitable private face, one that was created and shaped by the boys and ran like a cold, unseen, dangerous current beneath the placid surface.

At a prep school, however, the tacit acknowledgement of this fact – that the two distinct worlds coexist, one overt, one hidden – is never really established. The real world (the world of the boys, the hothouse society) never gets full purchase because there remain old elements of that unspoilt innocence of childhood in place – we were still children, after all, even though, at the end of our prep school careers, the embryo adult in each of us could be perceived taking shape.

I developed a curious relationship with one of the matrons. I can't remember her name but she was attractive, energetic and a little plump with reddish blonde hair and a nicely cynical, gently mocking way with her charges. I can see her face in my mind's eye, see her in her white coat serving spoonfuls of malt to the needy and malnourished, dispensing aspirins for imagined headaches. In our pre-teens the female members of staff played a far more important part in our lives than the males did. I can bring all these young women to mind instantly, have them fixed in my memory far more vividly than all but a few of the men. It was as if we unconsciously realized that here was the only likely source of any vaguely maternal affection – a smile, a pat on the back, a literal shoulder to cry on – which we all, even the most rambunctious and independent spirits, separated from our real mothers three months at a time, periodically craved.

Thinking back, I suppose that what happened was that this matron and I must have become friends, an odd state of affairs to arise between a thirteen-year-old boy and a young woman in her twenties, especially given the institutional roles imposed on us. Perhaps, quite simply, she was lonely. There is another side to prep school life which the schoolboy seldom considers, if at all – that of the solitary teacher in his or her room, little more than a bedsit, whiling away their off-duty hours. What did you do if you weren't married? I suppose there were occasional visits to a pub or a local restaurant (though the junior staff must have been paid a pittance); or you could hopefully attempt to find a soul-mate amongst your colleagues . . . And the social life of a staff common room need not necessarily be congenial, populated – as all common rooms are – by its share of bores and petty martinets, third-raters and sadsacks. This matron, however, seemed a more feisty and worldly character and, inevitably, she did not stay long with us, no more than a term or two. I never thought anything particular about her announced departure: she was popular with the boys and we were collectively sorry to see her go but, most unusually, before she left she came into my dormitory late at night to say goodbye and sat on my bed and talked for an hour or so. The other boys fell asleep or tried to eavesdrop but she sat close to me and we chatted in low voices. Chatted about what? I can't remember exactly – where she was going, I suppose. I recall something about her telling me she was sitting more exams, better qualifications leading to a better job. Did she kiss me farewell, squeeze my hand? I hope so. I never saw or heard from her again.

Otherwise the relations between staff and boys were by and large cordial and run-of-the-mill. With one exception. There was one young master, popular with the boys, who distinguished himself in our eyes by demonstrating a clear sense of his own sartorial style – a worn leather greatcoat, knitted ties, Chelsea boots – and who, we guessed, possessed a source of income separate from his school salary. He had his own car, something sporty, went abroad in the summer – there was generally a debonair and confident manner about him that we responded to. Then, one evening in my dormitory a junior boy returned from a late-night punishment lesson (malefactors copying out lines in a classroom) in tears. When quizzed by the dormitory leader he confessed that this particular master had 'fiddled' with him. The boys had been in dressing gowns and pyjamas; when this fellow approached the master – the invigilator of the punishment period – with his completed lines the man had slid his hand into the fly of the boy's pyjamas. The seniors of us in the dormitory – I was probably thirteen by then – consulted. We reported the matter to the head boy who decided he would have to tell the headmaster. We watched him go downstairs and knock on the door of the headmaster's study. In the morning the young master had gone, not a sign, not a trace of him left. A brief, bland announcement was made about his sudden departure, 'a family crisis' had called him away, and it was never spoken of further. We, as I recall, were

not so much outraged by the molestation as by the breach-
ing of convention: it was not so much the act itself but
the collapse of general principles it betokened – principles
of decorum and staff–pupil relationships rather than
anything more highly moral – this sort of thing really
wouldn't do. We were pompously pleased that he had been
sent packing and no more fuss was made.

Sex was definitely in the air as I approached the end of
my prep school years. I remember a very young under-
matron – no more than seventeen or eighteen – supervising
ablutions in the shower room, inspecting the fingernails of
naked, hirsute, mature thirteen-year-olds and, as I waited
my turn, I caught myself wondering if she found it a bit
embarrassing, standing there fully clothed with fifty assorted
sizes of cocks and balls on display. And I think she did.
Sexually we were insatiably curious: more advanced boys
were envied for their masturbatory prowess; there would
be the odd thrilling torchlit striptease cabaret in the dormitories late at night, and some more daring souls crept into
each other's beds for mutual stimulation, but their numbers
were few and they were regarded as mild eccentrics rather
than pariahs.

As the time came for our transition to the main school
a certain tension became evident in those about to make
the move, uneasy at the idea of exchanging a small pond
for a much larger one in which we would be conspicuous
minnows. There was a rite of passage that took place in
the final week of our final term and which symbolically
marked this impending alteration in our status. It was
known as 'P.D.' and was a one-on-one solemn discussion
with the headmaster about the facts of life.

The initials referred to 'Pandrops' – a name peculiar to
Scotland, I believe, which was given to a brand of large

round white peppermints. These the headmaster would feed the boy throughout his faintly embarrassed disquisition in the strange belief that the peppermint would prevent any unseemly arousal. Where he discovered this faith in the anaphrodisiac properties of peppermint I have no idea, but anyway, there one sat, dutifully sucking on a succession of mints, as he tediously ran us through the familiar mechanics of procreation. At the end he would ask peremptorily: 'Have you any questions?' This was what we were waiting for, the tacit understanding being that the headmaster was duty-bound to answer everything – everything – we wanted to know. Consequently medical textbooks, dictionaries and novels were scoured in advance for sexual arcana: 'Sir, what are the symptoms of tertiary syphillis?' 'How do you do soixante-neuf, sir?' The aim was to make the P. D. session last as long as possible, a fact which, rather than displaying the appalling extent of one's ignorance, was instead perceived to convey the impression of massive virility. There was a record for the longest P.D. – an awesome interrogatory effort which had endured for most of an afternoon, was abandoned and resumed after breakfast the next day – but no one in my year lasted much more than an hour.

So I left the world of the prep school after four years and everything changed, but my memories of that period of my life seem fixed and anchored in my first year at Wester Elchies; perhaps because of my coming from Africa everything about it was so strange and new and its impact inevitably left deeper traces. Recollections of my first summer there are particularly resonant because by then I had settled in, I had explored my world and was at home in it. And, I suppose, I was happy. It was a kind of idyll living in that remote and rather beautiful Scottish estate, for all its strangeness. I remember on summer nights after supper we would gather around the teachers sitting out on the grass tennis court, lounging beneath the cedar tree (or was it beech, or have I just planted it?) pestering them, chatting and playing, before the bell was rung and we were summoned inside for prayers, then bed. A wash and a teeth clean standing on the wooden duckboards in the washroom, then into the cool dormitory high under the eaves of the house. Lights out at 8.00, not that it made much difference, the thin curtains drawn vainly against the sunny northern skies. In reality I couldn't have spent more than a few dozen summer evenings at Elchies but it is that particular limpid northern atmosphere – the sun still stubbornly in the sky but the shadows long and with the warmth just beginning to go – that my memory most associates with the place and that time of my life. The ambience is always conjured up by Auden's haunting poem, 'Summer Night', written – coincidentally – while he was teaching at a prep school in Scotland himself:

> That later we, though parted then,
> May still recall those evenings when
> Fear gave his watch no look;
> The lion griefs loped from the shade
> And on our knees their muzzles laid
> And Death put down his book.

# The Hothouse

I have known few large buildings as intimately as I knew my house at school; after all, I lived there, day in, day out, for five years. All public schoolboys can claim a similar familiarity, but in almost every case you will find there is no nostalgia for the building itself. Apart from my parental home I have never lived in any one house for longer than three years, but I remember the shabbiest and most transient student bedsits with more affection. It is not all that surprising: the living quarters of your average public schoolboy are at best functional and soulless, and at worst utterly disgusting. If Borstals or remand homes were maintained in similar conditions, there would be a public outcry. I recently visited several famous public schools, and nothing I saw there made me so depressed as the dormitories and the thought that for so many years I had slept so many nights in such dismal and depressing circumstances.

It is, I think, a retrospective revulsion. Adolescent boys are not much preoccupied with personal hygiene, let alone the care and maintenance of their living quarters. But now, when I recall the concrete and tile washrooms and lavatories, the pale-green dormitories with their crude wooden beds, I form a new respect for the resilience and fortitude of the adolescent spirit.

Not that the conditions we experienced at school were the worst I have seen. At one school that I visited in Scotland some of the studies were in a converted greenhouse, which the boys had lined with egg boxes in an attempt to provide some insulation. Older buildings in older schools give rise to prospects of damp and decay that are almost Dickensian in their extravagance; the dormitories look like wards in some Crimean war hospital.

Anyway, we were fortunate, if that is the right word, in that our house was newish and made of wood. It looked rather like an army barracks, a large, single-storey, frame building, creosoted brown, with a tar-paper roof, constructed around a square, grassy courtyard. There were four very long terraced corridors with rooms off each side. One edge of the square expanded to contain a large locker room, towel and shower room and lavatories; one corner contained the housemaster's flat. We ate in a dining room a mile away in the main school, an old, rather attractive, stone manor house whose fine architectural proportions had suffered when a Second World War fire destroyed its mansard roof.

When I arrived at the school, aged thirteen, in 1965, everything about the house was functional and anonymous. The floor, throughout, was brown linoleum; the lampshades were white plastic. Curtains at dorm windows were made from the same drab material. Only in the studies was individual decoration permitted, but as this consisted almost entirely of pictures of women scissored from lingerie and swimwear advertisements, they too had a homogeneous air.

Prospective parents being shown round the house often found the unrelieved wallpapering of brassière and corset ads (interspersed with the odd film star or motor car) something of a shock, and from time to time the housemaster or the headmaster would initiate a clean-up campaign. Shortly after I arrived new regulations were issued. (1) Nudity was banned. Even the most decorous and coy picture from a girlie magazine (or nude mags, nude books, skin mags, as we called them) was not permitted: the pin-up must be clothed. (2) Only three pin-ups were allowed on the wall per person. (3) As a special concession, a fourth pin-up could be kept concealed in a drawer for furtive, private consultation. This is true.

It was vain legislation and constantly had to be reinforced. But as years went by attitudes relaxed, and by the time I left every boy's study looked like a Soho bookshop or soft-porn emporium. Indeed, in terms of fixtures and fittings the history of my house, and of all the other six houses in the school, was one of prettification and improvement. Carpets were introduced; studies were subdivided into cubicles or converted to study-dormitories; painting and wallpapering were encouraged. Taste, as might be expected, was execrable. I remember that in one of my studies we lowered the ceiling by two feet by tacking string to and fro from one wall to another and laying brightly coloured crêpe paper on top of the resulting web. In the five years I lived there the character of the house altered by stages from that of some sort of penal institution to that of a moderately prosperous South American shanty town.

Much of this home decorating was subsidized by profits from the house shop. This sold nothing apart from sweets, soft drinks and ice cream and did a roaring trade. It was considered completely normal, in the hour of free time between end of prep and lights out, for one person to consume, say, a litre of Coca-Cola, a packet of jaffa cakes and a packet of digestive biscuits, a Mars bar, a slab of chocolate, some packets of crisps, some strips of liquorice and a couple of dozen aniseed balls. Everybody, while his money lasted, seemed to eat constantly. As one rose through the ranks kettles were permitted and, along with them, 'brewing' privileges. By the end of my school career I was allowed a toaster. During an average day I might drink between twenty and thirty mugs of instant coffee and eat two large white sliced loaves of bread.

Apart from eating and drinking, the other memory I retain of living in the house was the noise. Certain periods of the day were radio hours. As if on command, dozens of radios and record players would start up. Very little classical music was played. In my era the sophisticated public schoolboy listened to Jimi Hendrix, the Grateful Dead and Cream.

We had a television (black-and-white) in the house common room. Its use was very restricted. Far and away the most popular programme was *Top of the Pops*. I am sure its producers have no idea of the profound influence and effect this programme had on a generation of public schoolboys. I do not know if it commands the same allegiance today, but I would wager that during the last five years of the 1960s 99 per cent of public schoolboys religiously watched the programme every week during term time. Everything stopped for *Top of the Pops*. In the entire school nothing moved. In our house sixty boys would somehow cram themselves into the common room to watch it on Thursday nights. And, pathetic as it may seem today, we didn't watch it so much for the music but for the girls in the studio audience. The programme was accompanied throughout by the grunts and groans, the whoops and sighs, of group passion. It was, I believe, in every public school in the land, a spontaneous, country-wide expression of terrible lust.

The house was large, but it felt curiously constricted. In the summer one could get outside, but during the winter there was nowhere else to go. Curiously, there was not much traffic between houses, except at senior level. Going into another house in the school was like going into another country, but with the added disadvantage that its inhabitants constantly drew attention to your strangeness. Few events were more unsettling than, as a junior boy, to have to deliver a message to a boy in another house. To be jeered at as an alien was the best you could expect; more often you would be set upon. We were members not so much of different houses as of different tribes. The houses all had different atmospheres, almost different ideologies. One house was corrupt, full of villains; one was full of eccentrics; one house was obsessively self-interested. My house, at least when I first joined it, was very hard.

We had had a succession of popular and ineffectual housemasters. There was no discipline. A new house-master was strenuously trying to impose his authority. But when he retired to his flat at the end of the day the old regime established itself. The source of the problem was a group of boys in the sixteen-to-seventeen age bracket. They were 'bad' in the sense that they had no interest in promotion. In the evenings they terrorized juniors with a kind of candid ruthlessness that I still find chilling to recall. They would roam the junior studies, four or five of these roughs, and beat people up at random, extort money or food, rifle letters and lockers in search of diversion. One felt in a way rather like a medieval peasant during the Hundred Years War: one never knew when another marauding army might march by, randomly distributing death and destruction. It was comparatively short-lived, this period of capricious thuggery, but it provided me with a full catalogue of the

resourceful cruelties of the adolescent mind. Later the
attitude of the house changed to something altogether more
genial, but I will always remember my years as a junior,
even though I was relatively unscathed. W. H. Auden said
he detested fascism because at public school he lived in a
fascist state. It is rarely a constant state of affairs, but it is
not difficult for private life in a boarding school temporar-
ily to take on certain fascist characteristics. It is the sense of
being a victim, or potential victim, that lingers on: the way
a house can become at certain moments a place of genuine
terror and fear; the way you sacrifice all principles in order
to save your skin; the ease with which the ideology of the
dominant group seduces you. This is, of course, the private,
unadministered life of a boarding house, but in a crucial
sense it is *the* reality of being a boarder in a boys' public
school. Its opposite is what I call 'the prison governor's view
of the prison'. That has a reality too, but it is for public and
official consumption. The inmates experience something
entirely different, vital and basic.

If you are lucky, everything changes at school as you
grow older, stronger and more senior. Those few to whom
this transformation and relaxation does not apply are the
saddest products of the system. But for the majority the
tenor of the daily round eventually establishes itself as
tolerable. However, the last year or two at school, although
the most privileged, can also be the most irritating. Most
people experience this, and no doubt most people have
their own reasons. On reflection, I wonder if my own
vague disquiet was not to do with a subconscious reaction
against the unrelenting absence of privacy that one experiences as the norm in a boarding school. Looking back at
it now, years later, I realize that of my nine years at boarding school I actually spent three years on holiday and a

full six at school. So for those six years, for example, I usually bathed and showered in the company of eight or a dozen other people; I relieved myself in what was effectively a public lavatory; I dressed and undressed, to order, in a crowded locker room; and, except for my final year, I slept in a room that never had fewer than four people in it and on occasions had fourteen. As a way of life – I am trying to be objective about it – this seems to me to be positively bizarre, not to say noisome and rebarbative. Five years in the same house is not only five years of crowding personalities; it is also five years of enforced proximity to the bodies that accommodate those personalities. The house was not a place for the fastidious.

Few people ever wield power as absolute as that possessed by a public-school prefect. Perhaps if you are an officer in the army, it may be similar, but really I feel it is more akin to something you might encounter in a feudal or totalitarian society, in so far as your power is subject to your whim. Boys may not be allowed to administer corporal punishment, but apart from that the head of house at a public school can – or certainly could – exercise a degree of control over the sixty boys in his charge that, day by day, could be said to be greater even than that of the housemaster.

The power operates on two basic levels. First, you can order people to do things: to shave, to repolish their shoes, to comb their hair, to have their hair cut, to run instead of walk and so on. On the second level you can deprive them of things: their freedom (by enforcing detention), their pleasures (you can forbid them to watch TV or ride a bicycle, reduce their pocket money, confiscate their possessions). A prefect may not be able to beat anybody, but if he works at it, and if the transgressions persist, he could probably have a boy beaten. Conceivably, if the circumstances were right, he could get a boy expelled. It is perhaps sufficient to say that, if he feels like it, a head of house can make the life of anybody in his house absolute hell.

I ended my school career as a head of house – we called them 'house helpers'. I was not very officious, perhaps lethargic might be more apt, but I don't ever expect to re-encounter that curious sensation of strolling through the house at night while everyone else was working at prep, master of my own territory, knowing that I could go anywhere, search anywhere, order people to do my bidding. It is, for those inclined to exult in it, a heady experience – perhaps not the sort of thing an eighteen-year-old should indulge in.

The occasion when one's power, as it were, stared one in the face was over the issue of haircuts. In those days all young males had long hair, and one of the stigmata of being a public schoolboy was the fact that your hair was so short. Consequently, everyone endeavoured to grow their hair as long as possible. The longer your hair, the more 'cool' you were. Haircut nights saw the head of house, clipboard in hand, patrolling the studies. His word was law – there was no higher court of appeal. Real dread was in the atmosphere. A local barber visited the house once a fortnight. He had to have heads to cut, a minimum of half a dozen. Who would be chosen? To enter a study was an eerie experience; one might have come to claim hostages or to issue a decimation order. At that moment the power one wielded was palpable.

A side-effect of power was adulation. They were not always concomitant, but one usually went with the other.

By the reduced standards that operate within any enclosed or confined community it was possible to reach a level of fame or renown similar to that enjoyed by film actors or pop stars in the wider world. These folk heroes had their own fans, even their own imitators. I am glad to say that at my school prowess at games was not the sole route to celebrityhood. It was the age of student rebellion and we had our own existential heroes. I remember a couple of them vividly. There was Burns, taciturn and poetic. His influence was widespread and was responsible for an improbable Ezra Pound craze that swept the school. Against type, he decided rugby was permissible and secured a place in the First XV. But somehow he managed to play his rugby in a dissident, rebellious manner too – brooding, never shouting, socks always round his ankles – so it did not diminish his *réclame*. Patmore's hero was Oscar Wilde. He always wore his duffel coat like a cloak and parted his hair in the middle. He would saunter around, carrying a daffodil, with half a dozen acolytes at his heels. I do not know what has become of these two, but from time to time I do encounter other erstwhile super-heroes and am always astonished at how bland and ordinary they are, and wonder from where they derived their early renown. The sad thing for these people is that adult life can never duplicate the fabulous triumphs of their schooldays – they peak at age seventeen or eighteen and it is all a long slide down from then on. They are the great reminiscers.

At my school promotion did not bring any great increase in privileges. Everyone wore the same uniform and rank was demarcated only by a silk flash on the left-hand side of the regulation school jersey. A house helper usually got a single study bedroom, and the prefects ('colour bearers') enjoyed a more lax routine. Baths were a great luxury. We had two to serve sixty boys, and a house helper's privilege was to order any boy out of a bath and take it as his own. There was always a huge waiting list, and because of the time involved the water was never changed. As a junior I would often step into a tepid bath in which the water was absolutely opaque from the grime of its seventeen or so previous occupants. As I grew more senior so my baths grew clearer. My one decadent luxury as head of house was to order the bell-ringer (the boy who woke up the rest of the house) to run me a bath in the morning. It would wait there – unused, steaming, limpid – until I came down to the shower room to claim it.

My own progress to this exalted position was straight-forward. I moved up through the various ranks to colour bearer, and there I would have stayed had not the head of my house been promoted to head boy and I was pushed up to fill the vacant role. I do not think, from the official point of view, that I was a very good head of house – I was too lazy to put myself about in the accepted way. My two interests at that stage of my school career were sport and painting, and they, rather than official duties, claimed most of my energies. I was demoted to colour bearer for a term for staying out one night during a tennis tour in Edinburgh. An energetic Canadian took over for the interregnum (I was reinstated the next term) and ran the house far more efficiently than I. Fortunately, I was not obliged to move out of my study, so – apart from a certain notoriety – the punishment affected me not at all.

Our school was in Scotland, was in almost every respect a Scottish public school, and yet a strong Scottish accent was a real stigma. Indeed, any regional accent was parodied mercilessly. When people spoke with a strong Scottish accent we would make harsh retching sounds in the base of our throats or emit loose-jawed idiot burblings. Anyone with a Midlands or North of England accent heard nothing but a barrage of 'Eee bah goom' and 'Trooble at t' mill'. We all found the mocking of accents endlessly amusing. This was part snobbery, part self-defence. All public schoolboys have an intensely adversarial relationship with the local population, especially with the local youths. To us the locals were 'yobs', 'oiks', 'plebs', 'proles', 'peasants' and 'yokels'. It now seems to me astonishing to recall the patrician venom we would express, like aristocrats faced with imminent revolution – a curious mixture of contempt, fear, guilt and jealousy. They lived, after all, in the real world beyond the school grounds, and however superior we congratulated ourselves on being, there was no escaping the fact that they were freer than we were – and that grated. I am sure that we in our turn were looked on as revolting, arrogant, nasty snobs. By no means a harsh judgement.

We longed to get out of school, but the outside world was both a lure and a taunt. It possessed everything that school denied us and at the same time was a constant reminder of the constraints and abnormalities of the society in which we were confined. Strenuous attempts were made to escape to it.

The easiest way to get there was to be selected for a school team. Because the school was situated so far north a considerable amount of travelling was involved in order to find reputable opponents. Rugby and hockey would take you to Inverness or Aberdeen two or three times a term, and often there were matches in Dundee, Glasgow and Edinburgh. Edinburgh occupied a place in our imaginations rather as Berlin did for poets in the 1930s. It seemed to our impoverished eyes unfailingly sinful and glamorous. To be selected for a rugby tour to Edinburgh meant happy hours in Thistle Street pubs rather than eager sporting challenges.

For the outside world meant alcohol rather than girls. Our stays were usually far too short and too well chaperoned to meet the opposite sex, but there always seemed to be a chance to get drunk. I remember a match in Dundee. A friend, who had left school a term earlier and had gone to Edinburgh Art School, caught the train to Dundee with two hefty overnight bags clinking with booze. After the match we had about forty minutes to drink the lot. The favourite tipple was neat gin washed down with a tot of Rose's Lime Cordial.

Once in the outside world, we tended to band together. This was because we were conspicuous in our uniforms (the authorities had introduced blazer and flannels for exeats to spare our blushes over shorts and knee-socks) but also because we were somehow fearful and on edge. The outside world was a welcome source of contraband – pornography, drink, cigarettes – and also, in a sense, fair game. When boys went into towns the shoplifting rate rose alarmingly. In the local Woolworth's two store detectives used to follow one particular boy around. He was the most accomplished kleptomaniac and used to take orders for his Saturday visits. We exulted in our delinquency and bandied legends of epic thefts: a souvenir shop in the Highlands left almost empty when a busload of boys cleaned it out; a boy who dug up copper wires on a nearby RAF station, at one stage blacking out the control tower when he sank his axe into a crucial cable. We would return gleefully to the safety of school, clutching our booty. And yet within the school itself theft was regarded as the most serious and antisocial of crimes – any thief could expect years of excoriation. Two worlds, two sets of standards.

Because of the isolation of the school we did not participate in the life of the local community in any significant way. We were too far away from most boys' homes to make any half-term break practicable. It was not difficult to pass an entire three-month term without ever leaving the school grounds. As one grew older this unnatural segregation became more irksome. My abiding memory of my final two or three years is of a sense of life going on elsewhere. I felt as if I were experiencing a form of internal exile. A few away matches with teams only seemed to sharpen the sensation of missing out, of being by-passed.

The school grounds were capacious, the houses scattered randomly about the estate. I had a friend in a house so far away – over two miles – that I could rarely be bothered to visit him. The scale made it logistically difficult to creep out at night. I believe this is something that happens in most public schools. Here, escape is indulged in for its own sake, not as a means to some illicit end. In our case, and to reduce the risk of discovery, the nearest safe town was eight miles away. To drop from a dormitory window, change into civilian clothes, cycle the eight miles in order to snatch a pint of beer before closing time, then cycle back, was too arduous to make it worth while.

The summer was always better. We were very near the coast, and it was not difficult to spend a fragrant afternoon hidden among the gorse on the endless sand dunes, replenished with food and drink bought from stores at nearby caravan sites. Summer meant tennis too. The school tennis team was a member of a league that operated among tennis clubs in that area of the north-east. We would play against clubs in places like Inverness, Forres and Fochabers. The great advantage was that these games were played mid-week, in the evening. There was something unreal about these matches. The six of us in the team would get into a minibus at about half-past five on a Wednesday or Thursday evening and be driven to a small county town. There we would be dropped at the local tennis club. The matches were so regular that often no master accompanied us. For some reason – perhaps it was to do with the nature of the league – we often played against mixed doubles, sometimes against women's teams. Here, at last, was life as most people led it. I have the most idyllic recollections of these warm summer evenings: long shadows cast across the red clay courts, the sonorous 'pock, pock' of the balls in the air, the punctilious courtesy of our game ('I'm not sure if that was out – play a let!'), a few idle spectators – two girls, a dog, a ruddy man with a pipe. And then, afterwards, in the small clubhouse, with the glowing, perspiring wives of dentists and solicitors, all of us still in our dusty tennis whites, drinking half-pints of ginger-beer shandy, chatting, laughing in the palpitating dusk. There was, at least to us boys, a tender, bourgeois eroticism about these encounters, which was much analysed on the bus ride back to school. We often got back late, well after ten, with the school in bed, all curtains drawn vainly against the sunny northern evenings. We felt immensely proud of our exclusivity and were the source of great envy. Although I was a very keen sportsman at school, I find it quite easy to understand why tennis is the only game I play today.

The two main vices were drinking and smoking. Drugs were taken too, mainly marijuana, but were not anything like as prevalent as they are today. Smoking was completely banned, drinking almost so. A senior boy might get a glass of sweet sherry or a half-pint of beer off his housemaster if he was very lucky. These drinking restrictions must seem positively antediluvian to today's public schoolboy. I recently sat down to dinner with a housemaster at one of our grandest schools, and the three boys who were invited seemed to drink as much wine as they wanted.

The underworld life of the school, then, was concerned almost exclusively with trying to procure and consume alcohol and tobacco without getting caught. Smoking was the most common. I would say that 95 per cent of boys smoked at some stage of their school career, regardless of rank and position. Like any law that is consistently broken by a majority, it became impossible to enforce. Most colour bearers – who probably smoked themselves – turned a blind eye. All they asked for was a degree of discretion. I remember my study overlooked a road that led to a nearby wood. Every night after prep I could see the hardened smokers, in all weathers, in all seasons, trudging off for a 'drag in the woods'. From time to time I'd ask them where they were going, to get the reply, 'For a walk.' There was nothing illegal about going for a walk. You could always tell the smokers because they chewed gum and reeked of Brut aftershave – a brand unanimously endorsed by schoolboys of my era for its wholly effective smoke-obliterating pungency.

Smoking was cheap, fast and easy to hide. Drinking, possessing none of these attributes, was consequently less frequently indulged in. Usually it took place outside the school grounds. Journeys to and from school at the beginning and end of term were drunken binges. Dances, school celebrations, open days and the like were also opportunities for excess. We tended to prefer neat spirits for speed of effect. I remember after one school dance a friend of mine drank half a bottle of gin. Apart from a euphoric light in his eye he seemed fine when he sneaked back to his dormitory. He was caught the next morning when he woke up in a rank and befouled bed to discover that at some time in the night, without his realizing it, he had not only pissed and shat himself but had also vomited all over his pillow.

There was a certain illicit trade in sex magazines. Scandinavian magazines that showed pubic hair were particularly prized and could be sold for high prices. One enterprising boy who ran the school film society for a term was sent blurry but lurid catalogues from blue-film makers which, as far as we were concerned, were the last word in shocking explicitness. Certain novels were censored: *Lady Chatterley's Lover*, *The Ginger Man*, *Last Exit to Brooklyn*. But what was permitted varied from house to house. As a fifteen-year-old I once got into fearful trouble with my housemaster because he discovered me reading Harold Robbins's *The Adventurers*. It was confiscated on the spot. When I boldly asked for it to be returned on the last day of term I was told it had been destroyed.

Apart from thieving, the only genuinely illegal act that occurred with any regularity was joyriding. In my house two boys used frequently to take the assistant housemaster's car out late at night. They would disconnect the mileometer and drive through the dark countryside for an hour or two. The owner of the car never noticed. This was an act of real daring, not to say foolhardiness; the consequences of being caught or of having an accident would have reverberated beyond the school – and yet it was not a rare event. All manner of cars were parked around the school buildings overnight. People would use them. The penalty for this crime would have been instant expulsion, but the staff, I am sure, never suspected that it went on. People could be expelled for theft, sex (homo or hetero) and consistent smoking or drinking or the taking of drugs. Few boys were expelled while I was at school: two went for having sex with school maids (the maids were sacked too); a small clique of drug-takers departed and a few heavy smokers. Boys often left of their own accord. Occasionally there would be 'scandals' that made the newspapers – boys vandalized a girl's flat on a rugby tour once, I recall – and also demanded the ultimate penalty. The boy who blacked out the RAF station also made the local newspapers. He was a simple, pale, gangly soul called Clough. He had made hundreds of pounds selling copper and lead pilfered from the air base to local scrap-metal merchants. The school, although properly outraged, had, I think, a sneaking regard for his entrepreneurial drive. His father, who did not want him at home, came up to plead for leniency with the headmaster. Clough's punishment was to dig up all the tree stumps on the estate, a task that occupied all his free time for about two terms.

Swearing was a minor crime too, naturally. It is perhaps worth emphasizing, for anyone who doubts it, that the language of a public school is as bad as that of any army barracks. We employed all the usual four-letter oaths with unreflecting abandon. There were not many nonce words or neologisms in our private language at school for some reason. Perhaps because the school had been founded only some decades before, traditions had yet to establish themselves. At prep school it was pure Jennings and Darbyshire – 'Vanes', 'Quis?' 'Ego!', 'Stale news', 'Cave', etc., etc. One exchange that I have never encountered elsewhere I record here for those interested in the folkloric side of public-school life. If you farted ('buffed'), everyone was allowed to punch you. However, if you said, 'Safeties', before you were discovered, you could foul the air unpunished.

We were obsessed with sex. I know this is true of all adolescent experience, but when I think now of the energy and relentless focus of our interminable discussions about the subject a sort of retrospective lassitude descends upon me, as well as a retrospective anger. *Of course* we talked about sex – we lived in a freakish, monosexual society. There was a parallel world out there in which the two sexes mingled and interacted and to which entry was denied us. No wonder our curiosity was so febrile and intense – and so destructive. The sexual apartheid to which we were subjected all those years utterly warped our attitudes and precluded us from thinking about girls and women in any way but the most prurient and lubricious. The female sex was judged by one criterion – fanciable or non-fanciable, to put it rather more delicately than we did.

Endless conversation, speculation, fantasizing, poring over sex magazines, fervid masturbation . . . there is something soul-destroyingly monotonous about that facet of public-school life, and one looks back with genuine sadness and weariness at the thought of so much wasted time. But there it was, and at the time it was the favourite hobby. We made the best of our opportunities. Every girl and woman who set foot on the school grounds was subject to the most probing scrutiny – housemasters' wives, innocent secretaries, fond mothers and guileless sisters visiting the school were evaluated with ruthless purpose.

However, the people who bore the brunt of our lewd interest were the maids. These were local girls, I think, and were hired – so public-school rumour famously has it

– solely on the grounds of their ugliness. It made little difference. Their encounters with the boys, three times a day at meals, were characterized by a one-sided traffic of sexual banter of the vilest and coarsest sort. Given the opportunity, more daring boys actually molested them – squeezing, pinching, feeling. The girls were remarkably tolerant. I never heard of any boy disciplined as a result of a complaint made by one of them. I think our attitudes to them brought out the very worst in our natures: it was male lust at its most dog-like and contemptuous, tarnished further by a brand of wilful class disdain and mockery that was almost dehumanizing. I dare say any male sodality – rugby team, army platoon, group of Pall Mall clubmen – can descend to this level for a while, but what is depressing and degrading about the male boarding school is the unrelieved constancy of the tone, year in, year out, for at least five years. It must have some effect.

There was also, it is true, a brand of passionate romanticism about our sexual curiosity that was slightly more amusing. Nobody ever admitted to being a virgin. By tacit consent conversation about the great day was always rather vague and woolly – it was just taken as read that everybody was, well, pretty experienced. There was one boy who made the mistake of confessing, at the age of seventeen, that he had still to lose his virginity. He became a laughing stock in the house. Little boys of fourteen would howl, 'Virgin! Virgin!' at him. He came back the next term claiming to have lost it in the holidays, but it was too late. His greatest mistake was to have admitted it – the only honest man among shameless liars. And it was easy to lie – no one could prove that you were not the satyr you claimed to be, come the holidays. It was quite important, however, to live up to your reputation on the rare occasion when the company was mixed. Many a self-appointed stud came to grief at school dances, for example.

There was also the problem of letters. If you boasted of having a girlfriend, some evidence needed to be furnished: a photograph at the very least or passionate letters. We liked our letters from our girlfriends to be as conspicuously feminine as possible – coloured paper and envelopes with deckle edges and illustrations and drenched in scent. Post was distributed after lunch in the common room. A letter was inhaled, fondled, groaned and swooned over – exhibit 'A' in the defence of your virility.

One boy, a jolly, rowdy person called Dunbar, used to exchange clippings of pubic hair with his girlfriend. In the dormitory the little tufts would be passed round like holy relics. We begged him to go further – the girl was French after all. At our crass, snouty prompting he finally did what we required. Together we composed a touching letter requesting a photograph in the nude. The girl was deeply offended, and the relationship shortly fizzled out.

Some boys, though, had exceptional good fortune. A friend of mine 'got off' with the Headmaster's *au pair*, a pleasant Norwegian girl called Ingrid – a fabulously exotic creature to us. Another had an affair with his housemaster's daughter, provoking fraught dilemmas of divided loyalty. The rest of us had to rely on rare opportunities provided by school dances or the biennial Gilbert and Sullivan, when the girls were bussed in to play the female chorus.

The school dance was little more than a meat market. By the time the girls arrived all the boys were well-fortified with alcohol. At the first slow number they pounced. The occasion degraded everybody. The Gilbert and Sullivans were more fun and more decorum reigned. We were meant to be rehearsing, and we saw the girls quite regularly over a period of a month. Courtship rituals were rather primly observed, and the alliances that were struck up remained for a good while on a rather chaste level – one was often invited to the girl's house for tea on Sunday afternoons to meet her parents, for example. This more sustained contact usually provoked the dormant, romantic side of our nature, and many of us fell deeply in love as a consolation for being denied any physical release. That came, eventually, usually as the dates of the performances approached, a sense of time running out – as with soldiers due to return to the front – affecting both boy and girl. These wistful encounters were not so shaming. They were like any adolescent affair – cute, thrilling, melancholic – a brief foray into real life. They ended after the show as the barriers of the single-sex boarding school were reimposed. The only real victim was the Gilbert and Sullivan, in my memory always appalling, for the simple reason that none of the chorus had joined for the singing.

Every boy who leaves his boarding school has been shaped and formed, like it or not, by his years in that hothouse society. Of course, each individual will be affected to a different degree, but the only effective way of resisting the legacy is to get out early. My generation of schoolboys (class of 1970) was entirely typical not only of every other school but also of the generations that preceded us. We left school as unreflecting snobs – we had a very acute perception of 'us' and of 'them'. 'They' were all the yobs, oiks, lefties and deviants who hadn't been to public school. We were also racist, in a robust, cheery, easy-going manner, as the blacks and Arabs at school could testify. 'Wog' was the commonest of nicknames and, to us, devoid of pejorative intent.

We thought of women quite simply as sexual objects. We were politically naïve – which is to say, knee-jerk Tories of the old squirearchical model. We had our moody rebels, true, but they were influenced by Bob Dylan and Jack Kerouac rather than by any political faith. I knew only one boy at school who claimed to vote Labour – we thought him a ludicrous *poseur* at best, a patent moron at worst. Although most of us had done 'A' levels, and the more successful were trying to get into university, we were afflicted with a brand of philistinism that manifested itself as a grave suspicion of 'pseuds' or anyone who was too intellectual by half. Also many years of group loyalty, to the school, the house, the team, the power élite, had engendered a mistrust of the individual – indeed, 'individualist' was often employed as a term of abuse. The maverick, the odd one out, the not easily assimilable, were to be regarded with caution. Not the best set of values with which to rejoin the world in the last quarter of the twentieth century.

So what happened? I think that, usually, the shock of encountering real life stimulated a hasty course of unlearning. Most public schoolboys have to start a stringent programme of re-education almost as soon as the school gates close behind them. This assumes, of course, that the society in which you are compelled to mix operates under different codes. There are still many walks of life in contemporary Britain where the transition from schoolboy to adult is imperceptible – the attitudes that served you well at eighteen will see you nicely through to retirement.

When I left school I went to live on my own in France for a year. The signal inadequacies of my education swiftly presented themselves to me, and I suppose it was then that I began to look back on the strange institution in which I had spent half my life and to wonder at it.

I often found the focus of my thoughts coming round to one boy, a little younger than me, who had been in my house. This person, a sallow, weak boy called Gibbon, had been hated by everybody, myself included. I have no idea why; he was just very unpopular. He was never really persecuted, just spurned. Sometimes a gang would descend on him, demolish his desk, push him around, but most of the time the punishment was verbal. He was a whipping-boy for the house. He appeared to take it in reasonable spirit, was not abjectly miserable, and so there seemed no real cause to change attitudes. He had no friends and walked everywhere by himself. He was so disdained that even other unpopular boys in the house would not associate with him in case the taint was contagious.

My own school career was, in a banal way, a successful one, comparatively untroubled and orthodox, but I kept wondering what it had been like for Gibbon during his five years. When he went home in the holidays and his parents asked him how he was getting on at school, what did he say? And, more important, what effect would those five years have on him as an adult? Would he shrug them off? Struggle on regardless? Carry them like a yoke? When I looked at my contemporaries, boys who had had a far easier time, and saw them, years later, still living in the heavy shadow of their school days, still wrestling with aspects of their personalities that were somehow corrupted, undeveloped or warped, I doubted, somehow, that old Gibbon would be the breeziest and most carefree of fellows.

# Memories of the Sausage Fly

The ant-lion builds its traps in sandy soil. It fashions – somehow – a geometrically perfect inverted cone. At the tip of the cone the ant-lion lurks, buried and invisible, waiting for any small insect to tumble in. When this occurs, the ant-lion at first makes no move. The walls of the cone are so smooth, the sand-grains they are composed of so fine, that only the largest insects can gain any purchase. As the smaller victims slither and scrabble on the steep sides of the cone, the ant-lion spits – or flicks – more sand at them, causing them to tumble down into the cone-tip where they are dragged beneath the sand and devoured.

The largest ant-lion cone I ever saw was about three inches deep; the predator itself half an inch long. I caught it underneath our house in Signals Road, Achimota, in what was then the Gold Coast. The house was built on six-foot concrete piles. Beneath it was sand, pocked with ant-lion traps. A lunar landscape of immaculate craters. Hundreds upon hundreds of ant-lions. A no man's land for any small crawling insect. Our particular ploy was to dig out a small ant-lion and drop it in the hole of a larger one.

I always think of ant-lions when I think of our house in Achimota. It is the first of our houses in Africa that I remember, though we had lived in two before that. At the time I was born we lived in a converted officers' mess, made of mud bricks and with a corrugated-iron roof. Achimota was about six miles from Accra and the coast. On the huge beaches, ten-foot breakers would cream in from the Atlantic. We weren't allowed on the surf beaches until we were older and could belly-surf, but there were rocky stretches with rock pools burgeoning with submarine life. Sitting in a rock pool, waist deep in blood-warm water, aged five. Life was good.

We moved away from Achimota to Legon, three miles further inland, to the new campus of the University of Ghana. We lived in a large U-shaped house, painted white with a red tiled roof. There was a large stoep, big enough for thirty to gather on, that gave on to the enormous garden and a view of the surrounding countryside – grass-covered hills, clumps of small tough trees.

The insect I associate with the house in Legon is the velvet mite. These completely benign creatures were the size of a fingernail, a brilliant coruscating red and did indeed seem to be covered in a sort of velvety fur. They were the only insects I've ever encountered that you could stroke. At certain times of the year, particularly after the rainy season, they proliferated, and the grass around our house hotched with them. My sisters and I used to ranch velvet mites, gathering them in their hundreds into makeshift twig corrals. There the mites would mill around aimlessly, square feet of shifting scarlet velvet, a boiling carpet of red.

We moved to Nigeria, to Ibadan, in 1963. Our house on the university campus there was long and straight. The garden was surrounded by a dense hibiscus and poinsettia hedge and was full of trees: frangipani, cotton trees and tall elegant casuarina pines. I would borrow our gardener's machete and chop at the frangipani trees. Bury the curved blade (made in Czechoslovakia) in the bole, which was soft and yielding. The tree bled a white milk that dripped all day. Later I bought my own machete for five shillings. It was useful for hacking things down. Ibadan is set in the middle of tropical rain forest, things grow at an enormous speed. I cut two poles and stuck them in the ground to support our badminton net. When I came back from school three months later they had turned into trees.

The insect I associate with our house in Ibadan is the sausage fly. It's not really a fly at all but some kind of bloated ant that grows wings and takes to the air after rain. The sausage fly is about an inch long, a hard shiny banger-brown, hence its name. In the evening, after it has rained, you shut all your windows. Wings unfold from the cara-pace of the sausage fly and they take to the air in droves. They are not very good in the air – it isn't their natural element – and it's as if they have only borrowed the wings for the day. They steer haphazardly for the nearest light. Inside the house you can hear them carom into the windows and wire mosquito-netting. Squadrons veer unsteadily around exterior lights. They only have their wings for an hour or so. The sausage flies touch down and their wings fall off. A lot of them die as a result of mid-air collisions, flying into walls and such like. The next morning the veranda is crunchy underfoot with their hard bodies, and brilliant fragile drifts of discarded wings lie in the corners. The surviving sausage flies have resumed their earthly existence and have crawled off somewhere to complete their life cycle.

My father went out to West Africa during the Second World War. He was in the Royal Army Medical Corps and was based in Lagos, Jos in northern Nigeria (where they grow strawberries and new potatoes on the plateau all year round) and in the Gold Coast. We have a picture of him, very young and thin, sitting on a cane chair outside a grass hut some time in 1945. He came back to the Gold Coast in 1951 with my mother, planning to stay a few years only. He remained until 1977, until he was forced to leave because of ill-health. He had contracted a curious and rare disease called 'Q' fever. He had been a doctor working in Africa all his life and eventually Africa was literally the death of him.

His work began very early in the day. He would work through until two in the afternoon when he returned home for lunch. He would sleep until four and then go and play nine holes of golf. In the evening my mother would join him and their friends on the stoep of the golf club (drink was plentiful, very cheap and on credit). Perhaps there would be an impromptu supper-party later on. There was nothing frenetic or debauched in this social round – it was a far cry from Happy Valley – but in comparison to the life that most of these members of the professional middle class would have been living in Britain in the Fifties it must have seemed paradisical.

They could lead this life because everyone had servants. My parents had only been in the Gold Coast a week when one morning they discovered a small old man sitting on the kitchen steps. He said his name was Kofi and he had heard they needed a cook. Kofi was our cook for the next eleven years. He and his family lived in a village some two miles away. In Legon our house had servants' quarters, a simple, not to say crude, concrete cottage a few yards from the main house. This was occupied by Kofi's son, Kwame, who was then in his twenties. He is now a major in a tank battalion in the Ghanaian Army. Kwame used to baby-sit for my parents. My sisters and I would often spend the evenings in his hot concrete room, eating the very peppery fried plantain that he would prepare on a small cast-iron charcoal brazier in the corner.

In Nigeria we had a cook and a houseboy, Johnson and Israel. Johnson was very old, his hair was greying, and he was very set in his ways. When I read Joyce Cary's *Mr Johnson* I always think of our old cook. Cary's Johnson is much younger but the two had much in common. Johnson had been married many times but had no children. This, he claimed, was the fault of the wives he had had and nothing to do with his potency. Just before we left Nigeria he got married again to a very young girl. She used to do our washing for us and when Johnson was away in the afternoons received visits from other men. Eventually she became pregnant and later had a baby girl. There never was a prouder father.

Johnson was very tall and lanky, Israel was extremely small and walked everywhere very fast. He was an Easterner, an Ibo, and during the Biafran War he joined the Biafran Army in order to get something to eat. One day he was given a rifle and five rounds of ammunition and was deployed in the bush to repel an attack by the Federal forces. He was always quite candid about what he did next. He took off his camouflage jacket (the only uniform he possessed) and buried it. Then he threw his rifle away and deserted.

Once, in some waiting-room, or at some station bookstall, I picked up a copy of *Scientific American*. On the cover was what looked like a picture of a badly made patchwork quilt, all greys, rusts and ochrous browns. I recognized it immediately as an aerial photograph of Ibadan town centre, without need of recourse to the theme of the issue – which was 'Town Planning in the Third World', or something equivalent. Ibadan is lodged as firmly in my mind as any of the other cities I've lived in. It is known, sometimes affectionately, as the largest village in Africa. It has a population of well over one million. Most of the buildings within its sprawling purlieus are made of mud and roofed with corrugated iron. The streets crumble away at the edges into large deep ditches and are permanently crammed with cars. From every house and shop, radio music blares. At night the buildings are lit with fluorescent tubes, predominantly green and blue. There is public transport but the most common way of getting about the city is in Volkswagen vans. When you see a VW coming you stick out your hand and it stops. You climb in (the sliding doors are removed) and give sixpence to a small boy who hangs on to the outside. The vans ply certain basic routes. When you want to get off you rap with your knuckles on the roof. The van stops at once.

I used to travel by this means from the university campus into town to the Recreation Club. Here you could play tennis, golf and squash, swim at the pool, eat snacks and drink at the bars. During school holidays it was a focal point for the children of expatriates. We would spend the entire day there. In the evening we would go to the cinema or go to a party. There were lots of parties. Parties in town, parties at the university, parties at the New Reservation, parties in Bodija. Teenage parties: the same boys, the same girls, records and beer, sometimes a punch made from illicit gin brewed on the banks of distant creeks and reputed to make you blind if you drank too much.

Excursions out of town were few and far between. Sometimes we would go fishing. Drive out a couple of hours into the jungle to find a slow brown river and spin for perch. Sometimes we went down to Lagos for a week to stay in rickety beach huts at Tarqua Bay. Fish off the breakwater, go sailing – dodging the merchant ships steaming into Lagos harbour; surf at the surfing beach, and at night sleep on camp beds in the open air, beneath the stars and a mosquito net. The Americans refer to the children of US Army personnel serving abroad as 'army brats' or 'air force brats'. There were times when we were 'colonial brats'. Lazy, self-regarding, pleasure-seeking and utterly incurious about the country we were living in.

That all changed with the Biafran War. I well remember the day of the military coup that precipitated the country into its civil war. I was due to fly back to Britain for the start of the school term. Johnson, our cook, laconically told me that I wouldn't be going. Why not? I asked. Because, he said, there's going to be a military coup on Monday. He was right.

When the war was on (1967–70) the tenor of life changed radically, largely because of the overwhelming presence of the Nigerian Army. From the minute you stepped off the plane at Ikeja airport armed soldiery became a constant feature of your day. Off-duty soldiers kept their guns with them: on buses, in bars, taking their kids for a walk.

One evening driving along a quiet road with my father, we turned a corner and passed an oil drum with a plank leaning against it jutting a couple of feet into the road. It was only when we saw half a dozen soldiers spring from the trees with Kalashnikovs levelled that we realized it was a road block. We stopped abruptly and got out of the car. The guns were lowered and the car was searched. They were looking for currency smugglers, they said. The soldiers were young and edgy. They wore the odd bit of camouflage uniform supplemented by their own clothes, gym shoes, flannel trousers, an Hawaiian shirt. Their guns looked very old Warsaw Pact surplus – with numbers burnt crudely into the stock. You looked at these guys, who had volunteered because of the free beer and cigarettes the Army provided, and wondered what was going on in the rebel heartland.

I haven't been back to Nigeria or any part of West Africa since 1973. I started writing about it in 1976 when I wrote an (unpublished) novel about the Biafran War. Subsequent efforts of hindsight and occasional nostalgia keep it very fresh in my mind. Particularly heavy rain, a warm and muggy night, the sound of crickets, a cold beer on a hot day, are always weighed up against their African equivalents and always found wanting. But it's the music of Nat King Cole that proves the most effective Proustian trigger.

It was one of my father's habits when he first got up in the morning almost immediately to put a record on a shiny walnut hi-fi he had shipped out from Britain. Invariably, the record he chose was by Nat King Cole, the first bars of which were greeted by loud groans from the rest of the family, but he paid no heed. He would stand in the middle of the main room, the sliding glass doors thrown wide open to catch the cool early-morning breeze and look out on the sunlit view as he sang along with Nat Cole. He always struck me in those moments as being a very happy man. Whenever I hear that distinctive dry voice I think of my father and of Africa in the early morning.

# POCKET PENGUINS

1. Lady Chatterley's Trial
2. **Eric Schlosser** Cogs in the Great Machine
3. **Nick Hornby** Otherwise Pandemonium
4. **Albert Camus** Summer in Algiers
5. **P. D. James** Innocent House
6. **Richard Dawkins** The View from Mount Improbable
7. **India Knight** On Shopping
8. **Marian Keyes** Nothing Bad Ever Happens in Tiffany's
9. **Jorge Luis Borges** The Mirror of Ink
10. **Roald Dahl** A Taste of the Unexpected
11. **Jonathan Safran Foer** The Unabridged Pocketbook of Lightning
12. **Homer** The Cave of the Cyclops
13. **Paul Theroux** Two Stars
14. **Elizabeth David** Of Pageants and Picnics
15. **Anaïs Nin** Artists and Models
16. **Antony Beevor** Christmas at Stalingrad
17. **Gustave Flaubert** The Desert and the Dancing Girls
18. **Anne Frank** The Secret Annexe
19. **James Kelman** Where I Was
20. **Hari Kunzru** Noise
21. **Simon Schama** The Bastille Falls
22. **William Trevor** The Dressmaker's Child
23. **George Orwell** In Defence of English Cooking
24. **Michael Moore** Idiot Nation
25. **Helen Dunmore** Rose, 1944
26. **J. K. Galbraith** The Economics of Innocent Fraud
27. **Gervase Phinn** The School Inspector Calls
28. **W. G. Sebald** Young Austerlitz
29. **Redmond O'Hanlon** Borneo and the Poet
30. **Ali Smith** Ali Smith's Supersonic 70s
31. **Sigmund Freud** Forgetting Things
32. **Simon Armitage** King Arthur in the East Riding
33. **Hunter S. Thompson** Happy Birthday, Jack Nicholson
34. **Vladimir Nabokov** Cloud, Castle, Lake
35. **Niall Ferguson** 1914: Why the World Went to War

36. **Muriel Spark** The Snobs
37. **Steven Pinker** Hotheads
38. **Tony Harrison** Under the Clock
39. **John Updike** Three Trips
40. **Will Self** Design Faults in the Volvo 760 Turbo
41. **H. G. Wells** The Country of the Blind
42. **Noam Chomsky** Doctrines and Visions
43. **Jamie Oliver** Something for the Weekend
44. **Virginia Woolf** Street Haunting
45. **Zadie Smith** Martha and Hanwell
46. **John Mortimer** The Scales of Justice
47. **F. Scott Fitzgerald** The Diamond as Big as the Ritz
48. **Roger McGough** The State of Poetry
49. **Ian Kershaw** Death in the Bunker
50. **Gabriel García Márquez** Seventeen Poisoned Englishmen
51. **Steven Runciman** The Assault on Jerusalem
52. **Sue Townsend** The Queen in Hell Close
53. **Primo Levi** Iron Potassium Nickel
54. **Alistair Cooke** Letters from Four Seasons
55. **William Boyd** Protobiography
56. **Robert Graves** Caligula
57. **Melissa Bank** The Worst Thing a Suburban Girl Could Imagine
58. **Truman Capote** My Side of the Matter
59. **David Lodge** Scenes of Academic Life
60. **Anton Chekhov** The Kiss
61. **Claire Tomalin** Young Bysshe
62. **David Cannadine** The Aristocratic Adventurer
63. **P. G. Wodehouse** Jeeves and the Impending Doom
64. **Franz Kafka** The Great Wall of China
65. **Dave Eggers** Short Short Stories
66. **Evelyn Waugh** The Coronation of Haile Selassie
67. **Pat Barker** War Talk
68. **Jonathan Coe** 9th & 13th
69. **John Steinbeck** Murder
70. **Alain de Botton** On Seeing and Noticing